ESSENTIAL
ECONOMY

ESSENTIAL
ECONOMY

RAFAEL MOTA

Rev. date: 03/06/2017

To order additional copies of this book, contact:
Xlibris
1-888-795-4274
www.Xlibris.com
Orders@Xlibris.com
744414

THE CAPITAL I BY KARL MARX
ESSENTIAL ECONOMY

PREFACE

Karl Marx explained the production in his book the capital volume I. He used in his book some economy element as the value for figurout the sales and prices in an capitalist society that he called speculative.

This book end in the explotation, he continue analizing this term in his book with another legal aspects of the capitalist society and he takes as example for it the England society where the capitalism had began.

Concernign to the value theory seems to me the he apply in some way the Ricardian value economy theory. This book analize the capital volume I until the terms the explotation of labor by the capital and ignore the legal aspects in relation of the labour worker condiction that Marx tried in the final chapters of his book the capital volume I-the production- as a labour explotation by capital in the slave work and the worker that had been working more than fifteen hours a day. That had been causing a society health problem and then the legal aspects began the attention in those labor conditions cases until become the legal reform.

MARX THEORY AND PRACTICE

The wealth of nations is charatcrizized by a production system that is in relation with the work, the capital and the land of the conmuners. Marx in the chapter I says that that commodity studied the wealth from a capitalist point of view in a capitalist production system; that appear the weath as an immense colletion of a "comun cities". That is for Marx an "external abject, a thing which through its qualities satisfies human needs of watevere kind" as an "object of consuption or indiretitly a mean of production". The concept of land, work, capital and consumption is in relation with the production that is all which that human beings produce for sastisfied human desires. The human desires are unlimited but that human being consume has limited but not on the human production; but in its desires when it is satisfied. Whatever that wealth concept it is about the nature that with its transformation of that human efford is conceptualizized as a production that is human in the efford to put in order the market process in order to satisfies the human desires throuth the consumption as the last way of the production.

Marx takes that as the Ricard value theory as a matter of exchange of "uses values of another kind" That means in the consumer exchanges of products or commodities throuth the commerce. Historically that human had a primitive way of exchange with the products, someone of then has A product which that another one doesn't had. So began that exchange through the value for a product to another products called by Marx commodities in order to satisfies that human needs througth the commerce. Marx saw that the human power creates that value for its wages in a production dimention of labor. The division of labor is about the number of workers that the fabric employe in relation with that called "time" by Marx in order to creates the policies of the profits of the capitalist fabric in relation with the division of labour.

So the labor relation and its conection with the production, The production must be consume in the last production process.

Marx established the value of the commodity with the human labor and production. This is subject to creates production and its wages through the human satisfaction through the consume.

The Marx point of view is the relation with the work that must be constant, attending the time hour labor that generates the capital plusvalia or what is in accounting the superavit for the capitalist or the owner equity-using this too accounting term in order to the capital that generates the interest of the capital profit. Marx also used the commodity terminology for makes some examples of production and value in the David Ricardo economy way (David Ricardo discovered the value theory when left home for to live his aventures of gamble-playing money so began the value theory historically). Marx says that that production is for the human labor as well as there are thing without commodity that has value without the commodity, like "the air that we breath, virgin soil, natural medoms, implemented forest etc."- The earth economy creates everything in harmony in order to be transformed through the labor that product its own wages; transform commodities for the production, market, value and the consume of the merchandises. The service sector of the production process creates value without commodities. Marx also uses the term "use the values for other" Under the term of the exchange of products in a historical society; example, using the utility as a term for the value that has not value thing that doesn't has utility in the term used value a a medium of exchange if the labor it is not count as labor. The Marx example is following "the medieval peasant produced a corn-rent for lendol lord and corn-lithe for the quest, but neither the corn, rent nor the corn-lithe become commodities simply by being produce for others in other to become commodities, the product must be transferred to the other person, for whom its services are as a used-value throuth the medium of exchange. Finally, nohing cannot be a value without being an object of utility if the thing is "eseless, so is the labour containted in it; labor doen't count as labour, and therefore creates not value". Marx used this medieval example understanding that the medieval system was based in the land property. the land produced the rent at this time. The existence of the feudal state based in the land property the national rent was based in this medieval system.

The land value depend at that time at its measures and qualities, that produce commodities for the labor transformation into a production for the commerce value.

Karl Marx commodity definition is that that "commodities comes into the world in the form of uses values or material goods, such us iron, linen, corn, etc. This is their plain, lonely, natural form. However, they are at the same time objects of utility and bearers of value. Therefore they only appear as commodities, or have the form of commodities, in so far they posees a double form. The natural form an value form" This is for exchange value from a natural material that comes from the mines like the iron or another the comes in another form from the land like the corn etc. this become from a natural form for to be transformed through the market and the commerce in the process the sale. Marx called the commodities that comes "into the world in the form of uses values" This is because the nature is the mother world that support us with commodities like all mineral, natural land production that becomes in form of mineral like the iron, silver, gold etc; on the form of linen that becomes from the land in the form of agricultural production of cotton or another form of natural production that will be called commodities as well as known by Marx like material goods.

Marx point out that that commodities in term of objectivity, observes the thing in the case of commodities, the value that means a value differ from the same sense fo the physical object of the commodities.

In order to analize the substantial social labor Marx follows the social evidence that appears in the social relation among the commodities and commodities. That means an exchange of value amongs commodities in order to trade the commodity value.

After the humanity depart from an stage to another the merchandises were bought by money. The money value had to support the commodity called metal that in the case of the nations support of money value so be gold or silver or another metal used for the nation in question for support the money value. Marx guilt to the bourgeon economics that "show the origin of the money form". That is also called by Marx "the development of the expansion of value contained in the value-relation of commodities form its simplest, almost inperceptable outline to the dazzing money form when thin has been done, the mistery of money will immediately happen". Marx is referring to the value in relation to interpret the evidency of commodities of defferent kind that is for Marx an extrenge "relation between the values of two commodities supplies us with the simplest expression of the thin value of a single commodity". About the supply of commodities is referring to what the society exchange as commodities in the form of money and not for commodity for commodity because will be an economic trueque of exchange without the value of money that is supported by the nation in question. Buy one commodity for another one commodity is another form of doing commerce because the trade of supply and demand in the exchange of the money value. That is concern to merchadises or commodities in trade for to be used in money value in the market, that is supported in measures by the nations in question in a form of exchange in money value in the commerce exchange of merchandises or products that will be for the consumer that what will be followed by the market prices.

Marx simple formula is as follows: a) the simple isolated or accidental form of value.

X commodity A– Y commodity B or Y commodity A is worth Y commodity B. (20 yards of linen–1 coat, or 20 yards coats or – X coats. Linen=coat is the basis of the count equation.-So Marx

Marx had a point of view regarding to the value expressed to explain that relation between the nature of the linen and the value expression of the linen and the coat. those became from the land and production. One form the cotton cultivation that is the nature of the linen nad the another for the work in the fabric that is the transformation of the linen in a coat that could be in the commerce in the form of sale that is the value that pay the linen transformation in the fabric in a coat and that will pay the wages in chain of production.

Marx expressed this relation like this: "do not plus the same art it is only the value of the linen that is expressed. And how? By being related to the coat as its equivalent or the thing exchangeable with it"-Marx is wrote it in reference to the process of the land cultivation, the process of commerce that is related to the linen and coat until the last that is the consumer that after a market process like marketing and advertising until the sale makes the commodity exchangeable in the form of value.

ESSENTIAL ECONOMY

Karl Marx in another point of view of the industrial value of products, tried the chemical and physical Economic aspects by its formula. He makes chemistry and physical formula examples and says "In the same way, butic acid is a different substance propyl formate. Yet both are made up of the same chemical substance, carbon (c), hydrogen (h) and oxygen (O) however, these substances are combined together in the same proportions in each case, namely c4 h8 02. If now butric were to be equated with propyl formulated, then, in the first place, propyl formate would count in this relation only as a form of existence of c4 h8 02. Thus by operating propyl formate with butric acid one would be experiencing then chemical composition is approved to then physical formation". This example of chemical composition made by Marx mean the extrasion of Carbon for an chemical product in the industry composition by the formula c4 h8 02 and the means equal parts of carbon, hydrogen and oxygen that will be an industrial formula composition for combustible, that is make by the propyl formate and by the physical formation by chemical composition that means the gas product. The formula means a commodity that is the carbon (c) that when is combined with hydrogen or compresed air with oxygen (O) in equal parts, by chemical industrial composition with the formula c4 h8 02 that that means 4 times the carbon propyl 8 times of hydrogen and 2 times oxygen could express its physical formation which also be the industrial process to formulate.

Marx says about that "this by operating propyl formate with butric acid one would be expressing their chemical composition opposed to their physical formation". That means not contradiction in the chemical formula why it could be dangerous in its physical formation. Marx says "values, commodities are simply conyelated quantities of human labor, our analysis reduces them. It is time, to the level of abstract value" Marx also says about the nature of the commodity "but does not give them a form of value district from their nature form". That express the dangerous that could be the industry and commerce for sell and made. So the chemical and physical industry makes the commodity in physical procure that is possible by the labor power in the form of work and value.

ESSENTIAL ECONOMY

Marx put another example and that is about, the process of linen in the industrial division of labor. where the tailoring works making the coat. Marx defined that as a "concrete labor" Also put the waiver example that says that works "weaving" to makes the linen transformation as a final product in a coat production. He didn't makes difference in the waiver work and the tailor work because the division of labor in the industrial production; that is expressed in more quatitities of linen merchandises. As an human effort for to make the final product in labor and value. So, this is the Marx example about the industrial confession of linen coat. That the work of the waiver and tailor transform by the industrial division of labor. That for Marx is in "general".

Marx makes reference of the human labor and value. Employment of labor is for Marx a "fluent state" in order to a human labor effort, in finding jobs for the creation of value. The Marx linen example is completed by a man in the human labor, in a state where the labor problems are solved by physical jobs in division of labor. The industrial production creates the orders of a coat value. The linen is transformed by the human labor in an industrial production of a coat, that is coming from the natural form of linen.

Marx also makes reference in a natural form of cotton that is used to made the linen in coat value. But makes differences in the lamb cotton and plant cotton that is used in the fabric for makes a coat. Marx said "this is the linen acquires a value form different from its natural form. Its existence as value is manifested in its equilty with the coat, just as the sheep-like nature of the Christian is shown is his semblance to the lamb of god". This means the sheep sacrified in the meaning of food, the sheep cotton and the fabric of a coat. That makes difference among the linen of sheep and cotton in the industry production. The sheep had another natural value in the production process. That is in the chaining of food, what is about the use of the sheep in the compsuntion.

Marx analized the commodity value using the linen axemple again. But at this time associate it, with th coat. "in order to tell us the labour creates its own value in its abstract quality of being human labor. It says that the coat, in so far as I count as its equal, is value consists of the same labour as it does itself". Marx tell us about the commodities value in relation to linen commodity that is equal to another commodity by the human labor but in the form of exchange. The commodity pass for a way of production and labor power that has another relation that is the selling value. Marx says that the labor "creates its own value"-that is correct why the labor is the first in the relation to creates value in the production process. So the labor creates the linen production in order to make a coat. Marx equation "commodity B with commodity A is the expression of the value proper to commodity-that expression is equal to the AB commodities and production of the value relation between the linen and the coat; creates by the human labour. Marx also says "the value for commodity B, has the form of relative value" This is the same to says that that commodity A become from a natural form and relatives values with the commodity B, by the production relation. But had been the value by the human labour.

About the quantities Karl Marx its first expresion about labour was "every commodity for instance 15 brushells of corn, or 100lb of coffee" That is the Karl Marx expression about truequing in relation to the human labor and the free exchange of the product called trueque. That express the human labor in the value of the 15 brushells of corn for 100lb of coffee the is equal but for the human labour value.

Marx continue with the coat and linen example saying "In the value-relation of commodities A to commodity B of the linen and coat. therefore only is the commodity-type coat equated with the linen in quantitative terms as object of value as such, but also a definitive quantity of the object of value or equivalent, 1 coat for example is equated with a definitive quantity of linen. such as a 20 yards" The same Karl Marx expressed this expression like 20 yards of linen=1coat or 20 yards of linen are worth 1 coat presume the presence. of 1 coat exactly as much of the existence of the value as there are 20 yards of linen, implies the quantities of this two commodities and the cost of labour in the same quantity of labour at the same time. But the labour time is necessary for the production of 20 yards of linen or 1 coat. It varies with the change of the relative expression of the magnitu of the value that must be investigated more closely. It is the sasme to say that the labour makes the waver in equal labor about the hours that makes the taylor in quantitites value. So the human laobur production is expressed by Marx in his example of the linen that it is transformed by the waiver for the confession of a coat that uses also the tailor by a quantity fabrication that creates the human labour value.

The Marx experience about the linen value change for the land slavy product that is paid after. Marx also makes reference about the coat remained in the constant labour production of linen. So, Marx plaged as an "infertility of the flax growing" "soil for instance, its value will also be doubled". The infertility in the Marx example is in reference to the improductive value of the work because the surplus is 20 yards of linen in 2 coat, why 1 coat is only half in 20 yards of linen in relation with labour. So the labor time is reduced and perhaps the labour will be have time for another thing like recreation. This is because, the quatitity of worker are employed. So that, example of Marx about the 10 coat 1 yard of the linen ½. Is the quantity. That in the same time will be the slavy employed. Marx says about that that "necessary labour-time be reduced by one half as a result of improve loom for instance-the value of the linen will be fall by half. In encordance with the equation will non read 20 yards of linen=1/2 coat".

According to the relative value Marx expressed in the value the commodity as well as is expressed the value of the commodity A and the value of the commodity B-He says: "rises and falls in direct relation to the value of A, if the value of B remains constant." So Marx point of view th value of linen remain constant, while the value of the coat changes. The natural form of linen depend of the quality of used production, the coat depend of the supply and demand in the market production that does not need the timer labour in sales.

Marx says "If under there circumstances, the labour time necessary for the production of a coat is double, as a result, for instance of the poor crop of wool, we ahould have, instead of 20 yards of linen=1coat, 2 yards of linen ½ coat. As a result Marx says about the value of the coat" sinks by on half, the 20 yards of linen=20 coats. So this production of coats depend of the number of workers in the production that reduces coat in the value market; so the seller had to fall the prices because does not employed the necessary workers for the production of a coat for obtain the surplus of money.

Marx says this "if on the another hand, the necessary labout-time be reduced by one half, as a result of improved looms for instance, the value of linen will fall by one half" So the Marx equation is 20 yards of linen ½ half coat in commodity A and its value in commodity B "rises and falls in a direct relation of the value A if the value of B remain constant."

———————————

Marx refer to the quatitative labor and the dependence of the producer 1 coat with 20 yards of linen depend in how many hours in that the worker had finished a coat why the numbers of coat produced that also depends of the quatitity of labor to produce a coat. That example of Marx regarding to the linen used for produce a coat and quantity fo labor depend also of the industrial division of labor. According to Marx "the labor time is necessary for the production respectively of the linen and the coat, and hence the values, may vary simultaneously in the same direction. But to unequal degree, or in opposite directions and so on". that also depends of linen quantity to produce a coat because the worker must be use more time to produce a coat thought its commodity value that going to pay the time of labour into to produce a coat.

About the example of 20 yards of linen=1coat, 20 yards of linen=1/2 coat. On this the time of labour is overtime why the poor cotton and the slow labor production. This is that the labor produce less quantity for the quatitity of cotton. and the worker has to work the double that is to say overtime to produce the coat exemplized by Marx on the value of commodity (the linen-crop of wool) it "rises and falls (Marx) in inverse relation". In relation to the commodities A and B it express the value of the poor wool crop=A and coat production=B. It is expressed also the overtime or the souble work time production that remains "constant while the value of the coat changes"-Marx. Why the linen value produce the rises and falls inverse in the cultive relation in the changes of the value of B that is the coat production by labor.

Marx put the example of the 20 yards of linen sayin, that the 20 yards of linen=1coat depends of the quantitity of labor that is "necessary for the production and the same proportion". That is why the number of workers employee had to produce a number of production that became commodities extracted from the land throuth the same labor that cause the cost of the coat. It is about the numbers of hours worked for produce the coat that will be depend of the number of employee in the industry that also depend that price of the coat that depende of the number of hours worked in order to produce a coat in the production of a commodity in an coat industrial production. So the example of Marx of 200 yards of linen=1 coat. So the value is equal to the price fo the coat after it will be produce in the industry and put in the commerce. The value of commodity is relative to the value and it is relative to the price in the sale and the division of labour that will be depend of the production in the market prices or in the value of the current money.

Marx in order to change the linen example of the commodity and value use the word value as an expression of value quantitative for that product that has to be equal or be similar in value for makes the value exchange. Marx says "the first pecularity which strikes an form is this, that use-value becomes one form of appearance of opposite value". Marx use the commodity value for exchange another similar value in the commodity work form. So he says "the natural form of the commodity becomes its value form but not well, this substitution only occurs in the case of a commodity B (coat, or maize, or iron, etc) When some commodity A (linen etc) enters into a value. Relation with it, and then only millions the limits of this relation. Since a commodity cannot be related to itself as equivalent, and therefore cannot make its own value, it must be related to another commodity as equivalent, and therefore must make the phisycal shape of another commodity into its own value-form". Marx try to say is to exchange the product for another product why it is the cost of linen for Iron, in a necessary exchange that determine the quantity of value in order to exchange the value that is so called trueque (A for B in the quatitity of value in exchange). The social form of exchange that what is so called trueque is the value, expressed in the form of money in the form of exchange that begin with the currency of money in an social exchange of values that is equivalent to the commodity for another commodity in the value of money. The money apparence is the equivalent that is not always equal to a commodity for another commodity in the form of exchange. within this form of value it is must be expressed in money.

Marx put the example of commodity for quantity. "5 beds = 1 house or indistinguishable form 5 beds= a certain amount of money.

For make an exchange of 5 beds=1 house has to be an equivalent value or be expressed in money 5 beds=a certain amount fo money; that is the value relation". That means that that productive labour commodity must be equal in the exchange in the form of commodity in the quantitity of money value. About this Marx says "the value-relation which provides the framerwork of this expression (about the up example) of value requires that the hosue should be quantitative equated with the bed". It is "essential industily" a Greek expression that Marx used is also ceses saying "there can be no exchange, without equality, and not equality without commenmsability".

Marx study the value making the example of the house and the bed like something homogeneous in the human labor and in the positive economy that is the contable time in the house administration. Marx cited Golle tha says "golle words ociuss that means house and memory but the rules of the dynastic interest administration" So, in the form of resquested commodity Marx says that is equal in the human labor and the labour is equal to the quality but in the form of values. The Greek society was founded "the labour slaves and it was a natural basis of inequality of men and of their labour-powers, so the Marx opinion about the human labour and the human equlity that was the discovered of aristosteles in the man possession, wealth of commodities in the social relation of equality in the value depression". But Marx considered it as a whole also as a use of value and a discharged in the value about what aristosteles said about the slave state.

Now Marx try some economic them like the free trade system with the argument of the French commodity as such as Bastit did on his thesis about the expression of value or the equivalent in form of commodity and money. So the money in quantitative "home of value". That is expressed diary on the stock exchange; so the merchandises and the free trade.

Marx critizized the mercantile system that in the sigle xviii formed a pre-capitalist society in the apparence of the industrial system that began the capitalist system in the xix century.

Marx expressed that "the the total expanded form of value of 20 yard of linen=1coat or=10 bed; tea or =40 lib coffe or =1 quarter of corn or =2onces of gold or ½ ton of iron or = etc. So the exhange of value in the form of money or exhange.

The Marx tap exchange of value hasa a physical form expessed in value in an organized society; that is a social eletrono of the human labour, that transform commodities in industrial labour. The product must present a quality made in the social expression that had the world interdependence in the development and in equivalent of value in the form of money or exchange.

Marx refers the antagonism that become universal the exchange in a burgeois capitalism system. Marx called etopia that production renlist of poverty.

Remains in Marx the influence of Fauerbach whose philosophy war in moral and ethic of the religion specially with chistianity influence.

The commodity value in transition has a value in the money form. Marx refered that mineral exchange in the monopololy expression of money and commodity. Marx also refered about the gold in an organized society that support the currency of oney in the form of coin with intrinsic value or the representation of value support by the gold.

Marx also refered about the value in an genealogical form referring to the human organ in the term of acromancy that is the skily or impection of justice of the human organ after death. This is in a productive estimates of the social relation after that commodity of labor use the value by the product that become physical in the impression of the nerve of thoreye. Marx also wrote about the exchange unit as an inedutive producer in relation to the private labour expressed in an reflection form fo that human life life from in an historical fosil of view. Marx called it hougers economics in the form of the respective production relation of the commodity production in an surgens sulfhat society in the sigle xviii. Marx refer also to the course of copies in the sell exporters in the relative labor in the determination of value, that put the agricultural exemple as practical since that producers corn, battle, yamas, linen and clothing in the form use. So it is the practical administration of the products and distribution-"the foundation of that formatives"-Marx.

Marx refer also the labour time that is the human hours in the labour transformation of commodities in relation with the value in distribution in the press of English society called burgouis in the practices of the industrial relation and monopoly. Marx notes from the Greek philosopher Espicusus (341-c 220 cc) that that human affairs, moral after Socrates the physical laws and atomon but human industrial in the indirect life. So the religion reflection in the real world of the "everyday life"-Marx. Marx also refer the slang of the industrial production. Also the monetary system with accord value in the form of money in an exhange value in the capitalist society where the diamond commodity could be exchange in value of money or exchange so Marx in exonale monetary system.

Money circulation of commodities.

The merme of value-The Capital I. Chapter 3. Karl Marx.

Marxim in this chapter theme is in reference to the gold sale in transaction of commodities and values, the sale and labour.

Marx analized the gold with the forgotten of the circulation of money. The money value is expressed in the commodities or products in sale in the market which the people buy.

The gold is in the market about the money bank emission that the central bank does in a country and them the people makes sales when the gold is the mesure of the money or with parity with another metal like silver, sterling or cooper. Then the people make sale, buy or makes transactions. The commodity is expressed also in labour because the production value of the product so the money value of the labour that makes quantities of products for sale, that is the final act of the commodity production so extractive for the final value of the sale.

————————————

Marx express the sales of the gold and silver and some nation suppor that bank emission in gold or silver. Let the cost is expressed in money sold prices. And sometimes the gold barts creates the parts for money and payment and prices agree with the difference of value of prices of the gold in relation with the sylver for makes payments obligation when the money emission is not supported by the gold.

Marx says "the prices of gold and the sylver which will fuietly co-exist a long as the ratio of the value of silver that of gold remains unchanged at 15.51". That completion is about the gold and sylver commodities at different prices. Marx mention also the relation of the pound of cooper but it is "vary change and some poor nation rations used it for living where the unit sylver dimes the cooper and the gold denies the sylver in the emission of money and the metal that is expressed in commodities values and prices".

————————————

Marx also its refer to the fluctuactions of the commodities in circulation and tellist a law of the relation of the gold and sylver with relation to the value, prices of the commerce of the commodity in the final production in the prices of sale. When the propels by extablish the supply and demand of the commodities of the values that is expressed in prices in its natural mesme of "value". The commodities are not exhangable in gold if not in its form expressed by the bank value emission for the gold prices in the form of money.

The owner proprietorship commodity its expressed in profit in the exchange commodity by money in transaction for selling and burgois market system. The commodities expressed its in multiply the products working day expressed in prices. Marx focus the money metamorphosis in the production process, its circulation in the evaluation process of production. Telletion is also antiethical because the money circulation in the volume when the security of production after three security crisis affects the consumer demand, production and the market affect of for commodities in prices in the value inflation.

—————————

Marx try to explain the function of circulation of money in an intrinsic value of money that is an established commerce value in prices in the market system. Marx establish the token in another metallic value that is the function that is agree with the cooper or the silver in the circulation value money with value in the exchange that "replace the gold in the current money in exchange."-The market value happen when the nation is in question in the silver uses or in the cooper emission of money in relation with the gold emission but in circulation money for to pay to the nation the debts in the iinternaitonal commerce. Marx also mention the credit money in circulation that is out of the money in the capital market because the interest of the capital gain that is supported by the bank system. The circulation of money that is borrowed in money or paper money that doesn't have intrinsic value in function in a promissory note for the payment that came by the silver or the cooper but doesn't be in gold-has not punity for the money to pay in paper money that circulates as a note of payment. As an example is the North America paper money that called dollar. Why doen't have intrinsic gold and has not bill in intrincic gold value in the exchange of the market value. Marx accept that the "paper money is a symbol of the gold-a symbol of money.

Marx its refer to the money in exhange in coin when there are some economic transaction in more money with prices value in the circulation of money. Something happen in the international trade with the money in exchange in the form of trueque that is the equivalent in the balance of money value in the commerce with another seller and buyer that gives more then another and this is not fair for someone or another in the transaction. So it is not fair tot ranslate the gold for the silver or cooper agree with the value or its value in its equivalent for obtain the commodity. For Marx it is "a social expression" in the gold value. Marx cited to Norman when using loser about the historically shame in another Europe aabout the "gold and silver is an incresease in value" and is hoard of gold and silver in charge or "variation" of value. When a hoard happen when the purchase is limited "because the limitation of money" There are not circulation of money or not the same account bout the hoarding in the form of money that is limited.

Marx explained about the payment between the seller and buyer. The seller sells commodities and the buyer pays in the form of money. The money is pay in the form of interest when there is a credit or creditor that lend the capital. So the debt or debtor payment will be pay in the form of money. For the seller, the circulation of commodities will be in prices when the sold is buy in the form of money. About the commodity hoard Marx says: "the hoarder in order to prererme the monetary for of this commodities. And indebted purchaser in order to be able to pay if he does not pay, his good will be sold courpulsory." So must be a shame in the commodity that he will not pay in a compulsory the sell that buy without a fixed price in the market, and that could be a compulsory sale. But will be contradiction when the hoard enter to the industrial and commerce crisis. It is known by Marx as monetary crisis. The intern revisions or depression or overproduction crisis where the money love their real value in the market system and the hoarding going to ask in an "artificial system" that means an speculative economic system.

Marx says "the fency bougouis drink with prosperity and monopotly entrin of himself, has put decrease, that money is the genral jouney margining cuativo" So the capital keep the quantitative goods for a better armonic fine in the same way that the good margin of the economic boom but with speculation in the deal of marginig because that keep hidden the commodities that the bell economy waits when the economy is responding. The roll is not the same and is going to be speculative economy in the concern of the money value in that kind of economy crisis. Marx says: "The monetary finance remains withing payments curve to be made in gold or on credit money, squales on bank notes:" So there is hungry money in the capital lease economy and the emission of the government going to be to the gold or in the parity of the silver or cooper that the bank note must be in equal to the parity in gold. If the nation in question in the monetary system supported by the silver and cooper. The drink Marl example is "example of the farmer that sells his what for $2.00 and with the payment of 2 buys a bulls for cash" That is true for to sells $2.00 loundry and buy wheat for $2.00 with the bible money that is in "exhange of money since leling in market in these transction naking by seller and burgers sin crisloling money maker value." So the farmer made a purchase with the money. And avoid an exchange of product because ther is not trueque because the wheat falls in the guess market. There is not real value measure by its commodity for to make an exchange for the product in the case of measure of he wheat and the salt book that is wasted by the money value in the market system non in crisis.

The capital establish the caracter of the money by the interest and this is for to expand the economy and truequing the debits to others in the form of money payment. This for Marx the "another hand, the formation as the system of credit itself exgouls? In the means of payment inhabits the sphere of large –scale commercial transactions"-So the circulation of money will be for make the payment debt to the capital circulation in the mix market with respect to the retail trade, a small scale in the government emission of money or without gold that the bank creates. It support the sale by money by the silver or cooper in the retail trade in a market sphere that is retagate the ceremony crisis as a result of the lead of money with the kind of results in the payment circulation. So the results of the taxes takes the form of money in the payment. That is for Marx for the "grows of production" So this process of the hoarding that that Marx consider "as an independent form of self-ensichment vanishes with the avance of bourgeois, of grows at the same time in the form of the accumulation of a reserve fund of the means of payment". So the overproduction crisis the capitalist makes accumulation for to sale in the balker times in the form of money.

The world trade commerce payment is leaded by the nation parity for the nation in question that doesn't loss the support of the money value in gold if the silver or cooper rent its parity with the gold for an international trade money value payment. For Marx the abstract labour there is not the abstraction of the natural form of commodities and the measure of labour by hours paying in the form of money during the trade that is make nation to nation in the world trade. The nation does the commerce with the another nation it is so called international trade. For Marx this international trade presence in the gold and sylver it's the parity of the sylver with the gold value in the trade of the mercantile system. The hoarding in the international trade will be the shame or an speculation. The balance of trade in the current money.

———————

THE TRANSFORMATION OF MONEY INTO CAPITAL-VOL. I-KARL MARX

The general formula for the capital Marx says that is the circulation of the commodities starting in the capital, but when the capital act is for make the investor in capital for to being commodities that put the market to sell and buy. So the circulation of the commodity that put the word capital in the market where the worker must be the people that sells and buy. Marx point out also that that labour is not pay by the capital if not not by the labour that creates its own wage in the circulation of commodities in the commerce activity. The transformation of commodities into money in the exchange of transaction of a commodity in the market supply. The demand for money in the selling and buy of the capital in the slang. Has an economy benefit that is the superavit in the accounting process or plusvaly in terms of economics. The Marx axis problem is the money, capital, money as such as the supply and demand. So the owner became the unical economy system so called capitalism or speculatism. Marx doesn't change the system apply for capital so the investment. The circulation of money gain the interest when is saved in the bank or its landing in money interest in money ciculation. Moss says cited by Marx "Capital money, capital is commodity" as the capital is money value so created or save and its commodity is in relation with the supply nd demand for the goods and merchandises. Marx almost reduce the labour, the supply and demand, sales in the labour hours for the raw material that out the commerce and the merchandises ways in the same labour that paid the teller by the sale and the production. Marx put the case of overproduction where the worker "produce commodities out of nothing, mercey zunig his own and logo"-"The capitalist desafront said monarechy investment of production" When the sacarcity is overproducing the industrial kepp the overproduction in stock for sale in a better tones. So the labor hour is reduced by the lay-off and unemployment. So the labout power in its productive equivalent that is the social labour.

Marx refer to added value in the capital. The agreegate commodities of production in the fabrication gain the surplus money of the capital. In another way will be an speculative production.

The value of the regular value is the percent aggregated to the merchandises in the form of the surplus value for the capitalist-the owner superavit or the boomerang main gain: so the surplus value of the production process adapted to the surplus value, profit earned by the capitalist at a rate of profit.

So the "nation trade profit is when the international trade makes that case of England selling cotton to the United States, India and Egipt". So the quantity of surplus value will be the capital inserted in the internaitonal trade with the production.

The supply may be sane or fall on the production process of wealth. Marx put the example fo the land and sea that he says not creates wealth and that will be in the form to creates rente a for of value in the production a wealth production in the fisherman. Unless in the form of the work in the production process in its form of investment aggregated by the work of the capital interest that simplify the value in the production production process so created by the labour that the sales by its own wages but the commerce takes the surplus value in what concern to the production process. The surplus value is in relation with the labour in a ratio. A different thing for Marx is an explotation of the labor power for the capital. The worker at beginning and futher years worked 15 hours a day and the slavery work was for explotation, illness hepenned and in England had been litigations in favor of a reduction of hours reduction of work and some slavery legal and human consideration. Actually the worker labour hour is 8 hours by legal act in almost all the nations and that was a worker conquist throuth the interenational organization of labor. So might be sometime explotation througth the production costs or by speculation.

US
ECONOMIC EXPANSION

RAFAEL D. MOTA

PREFACE

US ECONOMIC STABILITY

In January 1er.2013 The United States economy was declared in recession by the congress but now for April 23er. 2013 the economy market is in expansion with a 50%.

Happen that that US economy is working by the automatic method the treasury bank has the money that the Federeral Reserve Bank needs in bill to supply the money even for the deficits. Sometime ego the Fed had been buying sterling, gold for endure the silver so the value of the dollar as a current money with the silver or another metal aleation like gold and silver behind to this promise note of payment. So the inversionist are optimist about to invest and so the market growth unless the overproduction where the industrials recived an 50% in taxes for benchmark of its industries depreciation. The DJI is over the 14,000 and the economy has to be caution in its application why if there is not problem the economy will go get us to an automatic progress.

THE NATIONAL INFLATION

THE US GROSS DOMESTIC PRODUCT

The Gross Domestic Product had its base year in the four quarter of 2011 with a 3.0% enhanced wit the first quarter of 2012 with a 2.2%. So the data of the year of the constant prices increased in an annual rate of 2.2 from the first to the four quarter of the one year of the data base 2011 to 2012. Attending the data of the dollar value to the output of the market prices in constant annual rate of 2.2% in 2012 from the first to the four quarter of 2012. so to adjust the inflation distortion the value of the output in the one base one year prices in order to get the real GDP or use the GDP in constant prices. So the distortion of inflation is 3.0% that is the real GDP or the GDP in constant price. That is the GDP real inflation and actual production in the year. So the constant dollars is 1.0%. The constant prices is about the annual rate of the total output in the first quarter of 2011 compare with the third quarter of 2010 are equal to $-473 billion for 2011 and $-470.9 billion.

The real GDP in 2011 is 1%. So the increase cannot be due to inflation, since the prices were held constant in 2.2%. So must be in revision of the GDP made a new data that would be available.

So the ilegal business not report to the IRS and those activities put money in the market, by the activities, gamble. The economic decline for for more the two quarter, so there are an economy recession from the third quarter of 2010 to the four quarter of 2011 and finanlly the first quarter of 2012.

THE INDUSTRIAL PRODUCTION INDEX

The industrial production is compiled each month by the board of governors of the federal reserve system. So the adjusted and updated 2012-05-16 of the 26 major industry that are used to mesure the index after collected the data for the industrial production index. In this case is used in an historical record where the economy expansion and contrat that means when the economy is in recession. So the coicider indicator for the recession in the historical record is the 2000 thougth to 2010 and the the economy grew as little be in the 2012 in 97.4133 for the index 2007=100%. This industrial production was for durable goods, like automobiles, furniture and appliances. The consumer had beeen little money to spend that in coicidere indicator has tending to a recession periods, like 2007. The graphic coincident point is 2012 or is adjusted in 2012=100% for the each month observation. So the is a portion of the industrial production of the economy activity. In the historical data non durables goods where from 1950 to 1930. And since 1950 to 2011 the durable goods where the indicator of the industrial production index. The economy is overproducing with little money to buy and is in an technically recession.

THE LEADING ECONOMIC INDICATORS

The monthly leading indicators tell us when a recession is become. The data of department of commerce tells us about the decline for three consecutive month that tells us that we are wating for a recession. And economic increase also tell us that the economic will continue prosper. And an up and down tell us that is economy is difficult to interpret. So the indicators says the there is a slow volatile indicator-so the economy is slowdown and this anticipate a recession but we have ten month of recession and inflation. The data says the stock bonds and the banking interest is little affected. That means the government is expecting a recession but the recession is. Why the leading indicators has little impact in the bonds and in the interest when the economic is slowdown?-this is when a recession is underway. So the overall economy theory makes senses the spending and the market losses also make sense. So the people fell poor and spend less and that affect the economy growth.

In the historical record the leading indicators are forecast affect a little the bonds and the interest prices but the economy is slowdown and represents a recession and there are for the month of May, 2012 a fiscal deficit in the GDP of over more of $800.000 billions of dollars. So over here with this slowdown economy indicators of inflation, deficits and recession.

THE PURCHASING MANAGERS INDEX

Thte purchasing manager index studies production, new orders, inventories of purchased materials, employment and vendors deliveries. The vendors deliveris sales is also part of the 11 leading indicators that is reported every month. The purchase managers cover 300 companies and about 20 industries that contributes to the GDP by its size. So th vendors deliveries is unique and makes the change in the level of the business activities.

So the vendor delivery for the month of May was slower in an 52.75% in relation to the previously that was 53.40%.

However the economy is expanding because is overe the 50%. It is expanding in series constracting little be why the economy when is over 50% is expanding and when is less 50% is in constraction.

The vendor deliveries in series constibutes to the production, new orders, inventories of purchased materials and employment is convinced with five individual in series in the overall purchased management index. That is 54%.80 for the month of April reported in May 2012. From an historical point of view the current level is 54.80% Apr. 2012 in relation with the last year that was 52.75%.

So the economy is expanding but with slowdown cycles of a recession because the overproduction crisis that caused the fiscal deficit, the inflation and the unemployment. Historically there are economy constration form April 30, 2009 with a 39.40% but since Ausgust 31, 2009 the economy is expanding with a 51.40%. So the economy is expandig but with slowdown recession business cycles because the overproduction crisis.

THE LABOR PRODUCTIVITY

The labor productivity is compiled quarterly by BEA since 1982=100%. All worker data is called output per hours and for all persons and business sector.

The measure is like labor productivity=control labor output/hours of labour imput.

So the numerator is mesure by the total prices actually produced. And the numerator is obtained monthly by the total employment.

So the labor productivity=115,000/0.29 since August 2012=396.55172.

The numerator measured the price of goods and the distorn of the output. The denominator is the actually total employment from the payroll of various industries.

From an historical record the productivity is in 0.3% in the first quarter. That shows some ciclycal behaviour because is falling the end of the expansion because the employees will able to hire skilled workers. So the unemployment rates is low. the unemployment rate is 9.1%. So when the recession sets in the workers first go and productivity piks up again. So the productivity must be computed in quaterly output and finallaly analized in long term prices, wages movements since the productivity is required to keep prices increases and check the long term economy growth for determine an economy perspective.

THE INDUSTRY CAPACITY UTILIZATION

The Federal Reserve System collects the data of the industrial production and the manufacturing capacity. the capacity rate, manufacturing, the ratio of the industrial production to capacity. The data is collected two weeks after the month. That is shows the price stability and the economy growth. The capacity utilization rate depend of the money supply to slow the economic become in inflation and lower the economy is in an inflationary pressures.

The industrial production total index is 5.2%. The capacity utilization of the total industry is 1.0%. So the inflationary is in pressure because is lower. The capacity utilization ratio of manufacturing and the total industrial shows expressed in the percent of capacity never exceeds the 100%. This leading indicators value is good for the forescasting but for the overall economy doesn't have a indicator status. In the fed report the industrial production rate is 1.1% and the utilization rate is 4.5%. The industry capacity are available for a number of industries and products like manufacturing, mining, utilities, durables goods, chemicals and paper to name a few.

THE US INVESTMENT AND THE CAPITAL EXPENDITURES

The Gross Private and the non residential fixed investments were for the 2/12 427,5000.00 in the economic activities. It was adjusted to the annual rates The gross private domestic investment consist of the fixed investments change the business inventories. Fixed investments connects the residential and non residential investments. The mesure without a deduction is for consumption fixed capital that includes replacements and capital that includes investments by the business and the non for profit institutions. The US residents are the owner of its investments that not include that that the us residents investment in another country.

The economic activities were as follows: for the 3/12 430.8000.00 for the 2/12 427.5000.00 in relation of an investment of 410.000.00 for the 8/11 and 400.000.00 for the 7/11. Those economic relations were for the us investments and capital expenditures.

THE US BUILDING PERMITS AND THE HOUSING STARTS

The housing construction seemed to be in expantion when it fells to its highest level 31/2 in this year. the housing start to sleeps at 5.8% to an adjusted annual rate of 554,000 units in an economic grows from the 2005. That means a recovery in the recent months and that the case for March, 2012. The housing construction add to the GDP but fells in the first quarter. The housing activities has an oversupply determined by depressing prices. In the 2/12 the housing starts fell down 694,000 units in relation to 698,000 so reported, but the housing charged to an 205,000 unit rate at the time that that government debt looks like loosers. In March decline the housing starts to the biggest since the base year April/11 where the prices were volatile and the housing starts decline 16.9% in the housing permits and starts.

The means the a recession begin to shoop up independent to the recovery in the economy activity.

THE US BUSINESS INVENTORIES

The business expansion grew 0.4% in April/12 but the sales grew 2.6% and the whole sales 0.6%.

The inventories had had in 1.58 trillion in April/12, with relation to the highest on 2011 that was in 19.7%. So the inventories going to be to a deep recession.

The economic grew 1.9% the job creation and the consumer spending was in 1.9%.

The durable good increase 0.2% declinig 3.7% for March/12. The business investment falls 1.9%, the most was 2.2% in an election demand. Durable goods order rose 5.5 billion for an 5.2% in April/12. For the 2009 recession the order start 4.6% from the 12/07.

Transportation goods rose 2.1 led 7.2% for the commercial business in a rate of 5.6% in an historical data that dropped at a 2.8% in the order election that fell 0.6%.

That's were the business activities in order to pick up where there is expansion but a recession around.

US DURABLE GOODS

Historically durables goods become from the 1950, when the US agriculture makets, changed to the industrial market system.

But for the 2012 the variability is leading by times where the months changes as an indicators of the future economy activity that is used as an Economy caution.

For the month of May of the 2012 the durable goods rose in an 1.1% conditioned by the data of the two last months. So the durables goods orders Also was unchaged in expected orders that has an increase in the commercial aircraft orders of 4.9%, also in millions. For furthermore that transportation durables goods were excluded but the orders of this sector rose in 0.4%. Only the capital goods were good and that excluded the transportation sector.

The business sector jump up 1.6% gain of the last months since February and the order for April declined in an 0.2%. So, that was the market for the durables goods, in the economy activities for the month of May.

US UNEMPLOYMENT RATE

The monthly unemployment rate "involves a large number of people" So Gary Clayton and Martin Giesbrecht.

The United States had long time that doesn't meet a 4% even a 5% or a 6% in the unemployment rate. Now the young civilian force are trying to be incorporated in the civilian force after the baby boom economics.

This is very important for the states economies where the economy tend to slow event it in an state expansion, so the economy tend also to fall not matter the state economy will be in recession. The unemployment "moves" quickly. Historically is slow that could be realized and is in possibility of soon changes. So, the unemployment rate in the June to September quarter has the annual rate of 1.9% in the productivity that is for the year 2012. Also the labor cost fall in an competitive 0.4% among Jun.-Sept. of the 2012 and an annual rate of 2.0 over the year (this unemployment rate is applicable to the military unemployment rate). The unemployment is in 7.9% among the Jun.-Sept. of the 2012; but seasonable the unemployment rate for Jun.-Sept. 2012 is 9.1%. So, this is the quaterly Jun.-Sept. 2012 panorama of the montly unemployment rate of the economy activities of north America.

US JOBLESS CLAIMS

The US economy is in expansion for the 2012 November month. The expansion is about 53%; but the variable costs about the number of workers employed changed regarding to the level of production. So the job claims varies in the unemployment jobs claims insurance, that is the economy indicator. The indicator came in an slowdown during the expansionary periods and rise some months then the recession begins. So, the labor conditions must be in caution. The US jobless claims fall 355k a week before November 9, 2012 and that means that numbers of weeks is the average because it is the variation of a week to another, adjusted by season and that moves the average mesure for a labor condition.

The annual rate moves to an 2% for July-Sept. quarter; data that is different in comparition to the months of April to June where the per cent was 1.3%.

This is an overall indicator that is different to another indicators in order to predict the economic activities.

US-HELP WANTED ADVERTISING

The conference board is an non-government agency that collects stadistics from the newspapers since 1951. The conference board classified ads from 51 cities around the country. The leading indicators is to determine the expansion economy an the recession as well as the revision of the economy recovery. Also predict when the next recession comes to arrive, attending to the slowdown or diminishing economics.

So the data for unemployment is 73 million of unemployee that for October/12 decline 39% on the 50 states of the US.

This indicators predicts the end of the expansion several month month or before the recession but when the recession end the data is subject to revision. So, for October-Sept/12 the US economy is still in expansion and the follows up data will be the facts.

US PERSONAL AND DISPOSABLE PERSONAL INCOME

The current personal income treats about "salaries, tips, and hourly wages". It is the total income received by all persons take way the social insurance. The current and constant dollars is against the family drop of dollars in a business "expansion or business constration.

For April/12; June/12 and August/12 the personal income increased $19 millions for an 0.1%,. The disposable income decreased an 0.3% in output for an personal income outlays in September. So, for the preceding months, the personal income in current dollars was 0.3%, 0.3%, 0.2%, 0.2%, 0.1% and 0.4% in money disposable.

The follows data shows which the business is in constration.

US CORPORATE PROFITS

The domestic product reports the financial and non-financial firms, estimated in "manufacturing, trade, transportation and public utilities." Hstorically, quaterly, the GDP, received accounts in a 2.0% rate in the third quarter;, March 28, June 26, Sept 26 and the closed projected by December 20 in the corporate profits. That was reported by BEA on August 26/12.

The leading indicators shows the economy and financial health on the "corporate sector" If there is not a following data in the rate of the "future economy activity" that means an inflation and a decline in the economy activity. The BEA choices the general economy leading indicators for the future economy activity, for extend "the warning..in the direction series that may vary some..in the signal of the economy trend" characterized by a national basket and an international trend in the economy activity.

US CONSUMER SPENDING

The general consumer sepending is "considered important" for "the measure of the economy health". That data is reported by departament of commerce why this represents complicated data for the GDP because is disposable in tables. So, we going to trade the consumer spending that is reported month by month by the department of commerce.

The current dollar decline during recessions in an expasionary period. Manager gains a little during the recessionary periods. The constant dollars of the personal consumption get down forth month in the nine month recession period. If the consumption is stable is not predictable.

The consumer spending data reported by the department of commerce n 11/29/12; the consumer spending reports a rose of 8% in spendings for the 9/12. So the data for the rate of April-June period was an 1.3%. This data means that the economy earn a little for the four month in the recessionary period and earn a little in an expansioanary period. So, that the economy activity for the April-June and the September month for the year 2012.

US RETAIL SALES

The "series on monthly retail sales covers total sales for all retail stores in the United States". This data is published by the bureau of census "mid-month for the previous month". Those data may includes "buiding material, harwarw stores, automovil dealers, furniture, home furnishing, grosery stores, eating and drinking establishments, and many others". Generaly the consumpsion that is about 40% is "adjusted" for inflation and the current dollars in an overall economy "tends to go up during recessions but when the economy is adjusted for inflation the economy goes to pick up but if there is variability recession may be predicted.

The economy data is in revision for the 11/14/12 and the trade sales went down 0.3% and 0.5% for the Jun-Sept/12; where the economy is under revision for the recent 12 months. The current level is 367.56 B. and went down the last month, data that represents in months like follows: Sept. 30/12 368.66B; August 31/12 363.83B.; July 31/12 358.72 B. June 30/12 356.96B. May 31/12 359.81B.; April....So, the general consumpsion average from the data that followed up was about 37% that tends to adjust inflation and in current dollars and the overall economy is in recession or it will be predited and the inflation is adjusted but the economy is not in 40% for that time.

US AUTO SALES

The general overview of the auto sales is that that consumer expenditure is very important for the economy health. The spending is reported by the US department of Commerce with a montly rate, which has the GDP as a result for an inflation adjusted.

The auto sales is in expansion since 28 years ago but the rate for November coming from for the late best year 2008-2009 when the economy had a down turn of 14.94 millions and that was for the month of September of 2008. Now for the month of November/12 the purchase are in an 12% on the sales rate. The sales for Sept. are 15 millions of vehicule units. And the auto sales expectations are in 1.11 millions, 2.2% down since the 10/12.

The auto sales expansion is predictable for an "long term of trends" where the consumer behavior is considered as a change for the auto, because the auto agin - that must be replaced. So the changes are predictable for the future of the economy activity.

US CONSUMERE CONFIDENCE AND EXPECTATIONS

The general consumer is the consumer confidence in the current economy situation. Expectation is a a future about the current economy decisions concerning to spend or save the money and the both cases are called economy activity in order to predict the economy future. It predicts the next 6 month choising ages for the household income. It is also about business conditions "employment and income for the next 6 months".

The consumer confidence and expectations, so report on the June 26/12 are in the lavels of 64.9, 64.4, 63.5, 58.0 to 66.3, 62, 0. Those percent are for the month of Jun/12 to Sept/12 and to Oct/12 to Dec/12.

US CONSUMER PRICE INDEX

The annual inflation is used in the changes of one month rate where the percent change in the CPI for the recent month adjusted by seasonal variations. The Annualized means that a month change in relation to the inflation rate.

From the point of view; the US consumer price index increased 0.1% in October in relation to the 12 months rate. So, the index increased an 2.2% before the seasonal adjustment. The inflation, agree with those terms is 2.1%, on the national basket and the international trade for the month of October 2012.

US PRODUCER PRICE INDEX

The producer price index (PPI) is used to mesure the average changes in selling price. This mesure is used by the domestic producers for their output sale and this series is known also as wholesale prince index since 1978. If the price the price change in 500 industries as a over 3000 industries that incorporate its data, it separates the commodity price indices. The changes in the price changes it is the product sold by the producer. If there are intermediary involved the produce will be higher when it increase at the industry or factory. PPI involves goods and services but when it is largely it is ingnored. The increases in PPI lead the the increases of the CPI but if possible that that increases of CPI in the PPI will be in the imported treated. For the November month the US PPI index divided the good in decline of 0.2% and increase 1.1% for the 9/12. So the manufacture has a showdown of 0.1% in October and the crude goods has an increase of 0.9%. Finished good increased 2.3% in the twelve months that ended in October 12. The largest rate in output rised 2.8%, an increased in the rate for twelve month that end in March/12. The data means a change in prices and increased in the CPI in the goods and services sold by PPI and some imported trade are in the international trade wholesale price sold.

This shows a rate about a 6.49%. That with a monthly rate in changes makes the economy acitivity in constration because in those months the monthly changes doesn't excess the 10%,- indicators that shows the future of spending in the consumer economy activity. So inflation is in the consumer expectations, that is affected by the international trend in Europe; the slowing economy in China.

US MONEY SUPPLY

The FED put some money currency in the market that is called M1 or M2. As a store value the money has the power to exchange as medium of store value or holding money. The individual components are called M1 when are individual and the broader based is called M2. So there is an M1 outside of the US treasury and 1 currency in money outside of the US economy. So the M2 account with an M1 plus 1. In the national market the distortion of it, means inflation. So some eurodollar was put in currency abroad and M2 that is equal to m2=(M1 plus 1). So this data is for the October month of 20012.

US PRIME RATE

The prime rate is the quantity of money that that bank add to the borrower of its banks customers. The interest rate is based in the rate of money that the borrower must paid to the bank in interest. So for the October/12 the prime rate interest, current rate is 3.25%. It low per cent is for demand more customer, so the FED and the predominant banks, so stadistics filed by the FED. So the "banks can increase effective interest rates by changing the compensatory balance, the prime is a lagging indicator for both recessions and recoveries, So the change in the prime rate in normal at the time it could be takes place. In this case the FED is covering in balance the private baking prime interest rate for the October/12.

US DISCOUNT RATE

The central Bank, the FED is required to lend to another financial institutions. "The discount rate is the interest the Fed changes on these borrowed funds". The discount rate is a discret interest that when rise means that end of an economy expansion. Discount rate is also an official indicator of futures economy activities and another interest rates that may appear in the overall economy activity. For October/12 the discount rate was 0.5% in one year and strategically 0.75%. So the economy grew 2% in the third quarter. This monetary policy was organized by the FED in 1913 as a monetary policy for the discount rate.

US FEDERAL FUNDS RATE

When the Banks excess the balance reserve of the Fed funds on a short term, the interest paid is borrow, it is known as the Fed funds rate. "Most loans are overnight, although some may be for a long as 3 days.

Since 1955, the Fed history presents another interest rates in the economy as an overall economy activity but now the BEA classified it as a turn down "in the face of an impeding recession" as a leading indicator using another interest in the economy activity that is used also by the GDP for its future changes in the leading "indicators for the movements in other interest rates."

So the Federal funds rates for October 12/12 were 0.25%, 0.75%, 6.75%.

The weeks price rates was as following: week of Oct12/12 3.25%, month ago 3.25%, average 3.25%. So the Federal present rate. that it is for November month/12 0.75%, 025%, 0.25%. And for the 11th districts costs funds are 1.038, 1.069, 1.276. so those up are efforts by the government in order to impeding recession.

US TREASURY BILL RATE

The treasury bill rate is "one of the most important short term interest rate in the economy" Investors trade it weekly, for trade daily and it reflects the supply and demand in the most "current market". The T bill movements shows the comparison of the prime rate. Coinciding indicators means that the economy is turning down or that the economy is in recovery from a recession in an overall economy activity. So the treasury bill rates indicators was of following for the October and November months of the 2012 year:

0.27 bill 2 year 1 day 0, -2, -3, -3, -4
0.67   "5 year 1 month -3, -9, -9, -11
1.69   "10 years 1 year -1, -26, -30, -12
2.79   "30 years.

Coinciding indicators are for the 2 years bill and for the 5 years bill and that means that the economy will turn down for the period for these year and the relative data years, considering the supply and demand for the T-bill rate in economy activity.

US MARKETS, INTERNATIONAL TRADE AND FOREIGN EXCHANGE

For December 1, 2012 the DJI was overproducing in 13.02558; For an average of an 12,000 rate, the S&P was 1,416.18 and the Nasdap 3,010.24. Something about the trade deficit. So the deficit was 560 millions for the 2011. Why the consumer products of automovil. For the year 2012 the US had 2.1 in exports and 2.62 trillion in import. For the 2010 the US had 500 billion in trade deficit at the diference of 753 trillion in trade deficit for 2006.

The value of dollar cover the exchange rate, the economy reserves and the treasury yield. The US debt is 15 trillion, the reason that the dollar value decline. so the same for the taxes-the largest debt of North America. in the trade the EU demand so the euro increases.

The investors hold dollar and it decline. The exchange rate is compose of eurodollas currency. In the Europe crisis/12 the euro was 1.3463, fell 10%, and with the euro Grece debt crisis the dollar gain over the euro 1.32%.

The 10 year treasury rate yield was still in 1.98%. For the 2011 was in 3.15 and for the 2011, it fell 3.85%. So for the inflation the Fed put and M2.

By currency reserves it was in excess in Japan, China and the Fed put an M3 that means 3.36 billions in foreing government reserves in dollars in 2011. So the dollar decline because the oil prices.

Book II

THE RECOVERY ACT

The politicians enter in session after December first and one of the them was the recovery act. The recovery was signed by the congress on February of 2009 and it has the following goods:

1) creates new jobs
2) Spam economics by run to the growth
3) Government transparency goods.

In another hand the recovery act had been the goods of:

4. -Tax cut
5. -employment benefits
6. -financial contrats.grands and loans
7. - Has the goods for the chield credit.

For the 2011 the budget to give to the government was 787 billions. And for the 2012 has the goal gives the government 840 billion for expenditures and changes.

A federal 75% for federal buildings and 1 million to private housing.

That was he constristion for an government expansion. This expansion are the government efforts for an economic stage called recovery.

THE BANK INDUSTRY

The Banks are confronting many lawsuits that are about the security mortage. In the financial crisis the banks had to work with the forclosure where many homeownere losses its house. Another continued paying with the forclosure problems and regulations, preventions and the result in the investor of money in houses insurance claims against some Banks like Bank of America, JP Morgan, Chase, Wells fargo, Citigroup and others. The Bank industry was suppose to paid $1 trillion in securities backed by reclosure in mortages. The cost of litigation for the Bank industry could be in 300 billion in the case of looses the litigations. That will depend of to "find price tag, the costs could be lower profits and the slow economy recovery wekening the bank ability to limit deficit on market housing that showed life.

The Bank industry are stimuling the lawsuits in three fronts:

1) prosecutors who are accusing of fraud.
2) Regulations who are claiming to invest and buying in back mortages securities.
3) Investors to seek to enforce them "to buy back the source loan." We have the Fannie Mae and Freddie Mac whose monoqualige the real estate industry and were forced to be out of the real estate industry during the 2008 recession. So now they "filed against 12 banks last year, claming the denped the mortage finance giants into buying shoker securities". So the banks are paying litigations and the lawyer are "decended on a federal appeals count in Manhattan to make then case" ...The book foundation of Law by Joseph T Healey says "Perhaps the most important they to remember about law pertaining to property or real estate is even the settler errors in the chapting of lease, sales apartament or mortagage Settlement dominant case have potentiatly disatian results "The Bank industry whose sale minance during the financial crisis in the mortage of the lender did loan that must be paid in full until the release of the property. Investors can't force the Bank into buy back the loan because the unit land was for the property use and the interest rate of 6%. Statutarly or if the mean repay the loan it is until the lender has over the life of loan or is referring the borrower by 3 days to "back out the transaction" that means sign the document and retain it for the closing the document.

MONETARY POLICE
-BATTLING INFLATION

The recovery spending will increase and would be used for the business stability. That point out to an economy expansion, employment, on time income, prices and considered in the property spending in the limit that begans. Now the committee put to function the "Open Market Operation". That committee is integrated by seven members of the board of governors and firms presidents of federal income districts banks. In a green market there is purchase and sales of securities in as much as stocks and bonds. The government securities consist in bonds and notes that that sale is not and will by financial millions and the government. The open market comitee put the prices that increase faster and then is necessary to stop the inflationary economic trend. The federal resources beings by the Treasury securitites for stimulate the growth for the 2013. The fed is buying bonds hoping that that market improve. The economic recovery is about of millios of people looking for work and the fed is working to improve it. But there is not too much optimism about the practice of scheduled the tax increase and spending that that in the next year would be working in the units efforts and played the economic back into a recession.

The federal open market committee is hoping a new monthly policy by Bernake. The monthly policy must creates money by crediting banks accounts that sells bonds to the fed. The same method apologized for the mortage bonds that that fed will be selling by a quantitative method. that must reduce the deficit in long term, taking in account the efforts-so Bernake. The bonds are issue by the Treasury in online for to pay in current as a part of the government defecit. The fed bought millios of bonds in an open market operative firm permited by the banks. The fed wants to increase the bonds reserves generates the banks by the amount of purchase.

THE FISCAL POLICY

Republicans and Democrats were discussing the fiscal policy in the congress. Democrats wanted more spending from the government on an long expansionary policy and the Republicans wanted an economic contraction in the federal act in order to take control of the inflation.

So the economic grew 2.2 for the 12/13 and decrease 2.1 for the same month. The job market was 6.5% in the holidays season.

Barack Obama wanted a tax cut to 250,000 salaries and republicans wanted to make the cuts to the over 1,000.000 wages.

But those fiscal policy doesn't muchin an increase of wages concerning to export increase. Something pending about the imports, China and Japon had been dollars in over about the arancel that coud be in the market in the economic recession expecualtion borrow. The congress decided after all to charge the wages of 450,000 b. This fiscal policy was for combat the inflation.

THE FISCAL CEILING

The US debt is over 10 trillion dollars and government wanted more money for to cover the fiscal deficit. So the trasury declared that the bank can't supply more money to the government.

So the fed invested 1 trillion in platinum in order to make strongest the dollar in the exchange international trend. That was in telatioin to houses or bushels that are as regulation in the international relations.

The platinum support the silver in the parity with the gold. Germany put a ton of gold in Fed in order to do business in the money parity that what need the US monetary policy. So at the time 1/13/13 Germany doen't know the monetary effect in the US in working economy but belives in an strongest help in the money supply to control a world economy in difficulties.

THE MONETARY ESTIMEED

By January 21, 2013 the US is passing for a debt crisis, overproduction and a declared recession in the economic trend. The Europe contries are taking out of the crisis at the time that Germany is in recession with a political election where makel is running for a third mandate. So the world economy is money out to globalization. The import and export are subjet to money currency estimated, where the gold put in order the silver, the sterling in the international market division of labour, where the currency now is extimeed in export waighter international economy. The US has a deficit of 16.9 trillion dollars in debt, that is expenditures now in the national buget crisis. Now Geremany try to put 3 trillion of gold in the US. England and France with the problem for Germany in order to translate the gold bar to New York. The sterling or platinum put in the market by the fed fiscal policy in order to reduce the fiscal policy and for reduce the debt of the fiscal deficit The Bank bank are in the limit of 16.4 trillion without a congress permission. The world is in an international currency war, where the japon is growing and expect an inflation. Also is short with 13 dollars less between the jen and dollar currency exchange for Jan.12/13.

US DEBT LIMIT

The government had a debt limit of 16.4 and the congress in a reunion on Jan. 21/13 approve a buget of 84 billions that may reduced the same session I 24 billions.

The treasury estimate the position of the congress in order to borrow the money until May 201e. The Pentagon decline bond budget that was reduced to 7.4% where the works with cut of 5.2% that means a 2.2% of the budget act. The economy is in deficit in a recession in the current economic cycles for January 2013. So the economy trend obey the GNP international trend or in the international corporations market. The congress expect to resolve the deficit in a large permit the debt of 102 yan in millions. The may collect 600 million in taxes. The congress vote to borrow money for the debt, the mean for the treasury weighest-that means a monetry policy with the silver and the gold in the currency money; looking caution and corned sterling (platinum) with an international value of cooper that China may wargected in the international trade.

Overproduction is used in the US and after that that government budget the money, the industry has to regulate the prices and the inflation; establishing the deflation in the currency policy to solve the prices.

So the government must paid in May 2013. The economy was declared in recession, with a recessionary cycle but also declared in growth that means that that GNP is leading to the progress (an big decline in the production may enter the US economy in a depression but in the contrary the economy will be leading to GNP for the progress in the business cycles, now in recession).

POST-DATA

During the four month recession The US control the crisis (the became from January first, 2013) by the automatic method, until the economic entered to the expansion and growth in April 16, 2013. During the automatic method the US economic was in stabilization making control of the economic fluctuations and the progressive taxes that became from the national rent and the recession facts of monetary worker compensation for unemployment.

So happened during the production indexes of overproduction.

For the month of May, 2013 the economic grows was 2.5. The expansion was in the 50% with the production over the 15,000 and with $20.00 dollars for the diary spending. That showed and economic stability in the U.S. economy.

US ECONOMIC TREND

After the actual GNP progress, the US economic had been slowdown on an GNP trend called in Recession. But, it is a time of overproduction, the Down Jones had been increased to a record average, that is over of the 16,000. It is normal that in the time of overproduction appears unemployment, recession and another social problems.

But now the real estate is doing good, the bank industry had been doing good also but it is dangerous for the US Economic at this time that the bank policy tried to catch all in an industrial manufacture production that has to wait an agricultural production for to makes its economic equilibrium.

The unemployment seems going to be reduced

And the real estate goes to increase at the time that the bank going to reduce its operations.

Also it's a time of a government policy where the industrial investor doesn't like to know of inflation or deflation in the economy.

At the actual GNP the monopolies tried to make an equilibrium in the supply and demand attending the overproduction, trying the demand for the consumption. Now, the consumption is slowdown for an GNP trend in recession.

So, at this point the government will place in the market an economic stimulus.

THE UNEMPLOYMENT BENEFITS EXTENTION

The inferior and the superior congress are discussing without result the unemployment extention benefits for the worker.

The majority of those people were unemployed for about six month and when found a job, the time of work duration are not more then two month.

The industry in other words are reducing the hours of work.

The overproduction is pointing out a reduction of work why is possible that the industry had the industrial production in stock because to an slowdown in the consumption.

However is also possible that will be a reduction of unemployment because the banks will have to reduce the interest rate for the industrial investment, that has to creates jobs for the worker.

The manufacture industry didn't receive during the financial crisis the benchmark money but a 50% in its income tax.

We must remember that during the George Bush father the unemployment extension benefits were about for three years because the recession of the Persian Gulf War why the military expenses. In the real estate doesn't know yet if Freddy Mae or Fanny Mae has been the capital to invest. So the government had been to put capital as a lender or an investor through buying bonds.

My point is that the unemployment will be reduced as a result of the land and capital on the economy scenery of the labour.

Another point is the ObamaCare that was a result of the social security reduction and that dislike the US political and economy panorama.

POST-DATA:
THE POST CRISIS

The economic turned back to the GNP Trend progress after an economy slowdown. The monopolies or big businees are doing good but only Macys report a cut for January 8, 2014.

Book III

US FINANCIAL CRASH

THE US HIGH INCOME

The one year of labor and property in the usa are located on the resources of 2015 and the proyected years of 2016 and 2017 are as follows:

2015=2.8
2016=3.3
2017=3.2

On this financial study the end of the 2015 with a 2.8 in the high income will be interesting for the 2016 year that could be growth in the proyection in 3.3 in the usa labor market and resources.

But and so the world bank projection about it; in 2017 the labor (wages) high income and resources will be low on 3.2 in relation to the year of 2016.

Those labor and resources are located in the $200.000.00 wages according to the US GROWTH where the middle class salaries desapare until the financial crisis of the years 2007-2009, however the economy recovery of the years 2010-2012 and the years of 2013-2015. So, for the base year of 2016 are also projected an final crash that seems the couln't be affect the $200,000.00 labor high income wages after the desaparence of the middle class that for many years were the back bone consumers of the US economy.

THE INFLATION

The consumer inflation was as following.

7/15=0.20
2016=2.10
2017=2.30

So, the economist intelligence unit the change in those per cent growing up by the base year 2016 and the following year 2017.

90 million people are unemployed in the usa economy and are food stamp recipient in the national basket on the growth economy.

MARKET GOLD PRICE AND THE UNEMPLOYMENT CLAIMS

So, data of Market Pulse in the closing year 2015 (that means December 31 of the same year) the gold price close in 1060 dollars and from the same source the unemployment claims for the end of the year were 237k.

Investors are investing in gold since an microeconomics point of view why they considers that the dollar will become most stronger.

And from a data of Investor-more then 90 million people are unemployed in the usa economy-that takes food stamps.

But from a Macroeconomics point o view the economic problem seems to see another.

I have mention about the new monetary system adapted for the FMI to the usa economics-were will a substitution in the current money dollar bill for another money bill that is not yet in the money market.

An crazy case is the silver market price that in 2015 had sold at $14 dollars oz. So that is happening with the silver is that it end in the mine-no more silver-it finito so a t.v. report in Spanish by the history channel about the silver. The usa had its monetary system parity supported by the silver that had an international gold value a little over to the 3.80.

So, in the usa money panorama investor are investing in gold knowing of its control of the market with 20% in investment-the another 80% belong to the small business.

Multinationals from my point of view must accept the new macroeconomic problem that face America.

US INVESTMENT SPENDING COULD BE TRACT IN 2016

The investment expenditure was in a lower 11% on relation to the 2014 and the 2015 year. Of the 500 s&p companies only there are 255 companies working in investment.

The usa oil industry had decrese in 47% in the 2015.

So, the 2015 economy shows a recession of then more four quarter that is known as a financial crash for 2016 a base year that project the 2017 year.

The international 500 s&p index is in poor index why 255 companies has the capital in order to spend in investment.

The texas oil that was selling almost an usa reserve oil at 40 dollars the oil barril and that decrese 47% in 2015 and are not projected by the 2016, where there is not too much to say because that what is spected is a financial crash for the 2016 year as a consecuence to the 2015 recession.

Multinationals had been in control of the usa economy putting in practice the supply economy theory in order to established an overproduction economy in the usa that jumped since that 14,000 record to the 17,000 in the DJI.

So, investors are not seeing profit the market in global competition markets and where they has to fight with the government proctetionism that had had not many choices to the free trade.

US SPENDING, SALES AND EXPECTATIONS

The manufacturing index is in 51.3 in expectations with a lowest sale expectation of 28%.

In a speculative market only 2000 industry are operating with 1.000.000 million in Bank deposit.

But the economy problem continue in a historical gold spending and to the same time a desilution about the silver price-now with a 2.50 market price.

The mines are in a risk-so global investors. And they see a lowest expectation in the usa economy for the 2016.

The investors are the loosing the they had been in investment.

Some world mines was touched by investors but without success.

Another economy problem that investor see is the wether. They study the sale though the el nino-small sales that are not why the change in wether but for a supply economy and for an overproduction economies that on an international order had been an external debt over the 18 trillion dollars. Also by an Obama proctetion economics tending to the left.

Note: The Obama administration put $400 billion in favor to the investors at the beginning of his presidency. During the 2007-09 crisis the investors received an 50% for the benchmark but the us army forces are spending 50 million by minutes in the war. However exist an investor internal liabilities and also an internal debt.

US MONEY VALUE AND EXCHANGE

On the 12-31-15 the money exchange value in relation with the Euro was 0.97 cents and 0.94 cents.

And for 1-5-16 the silver was on usd 13.31 that in relation with the euro was 12.74 but in currency value (in price) was 1.24-so merril edge data.

The silver money value price is about what can buy the dollar. That is why the silver covertion for the dollar value price and exchange.

US FINANCIAL INTERNATIONAL TRADE

So, data from US census the usa economy had been a deficit of 43.9 billion and in relation with the us export had a low balance of 42,5 billion. This data of the usa census is dated on the 12-4-15.

In the usa economy had been a lower export in relation with that usa buy in the foreing markets. The industrial production why that above reduced its production and that was refleted in the usa economy with unemployment. The us left government capitalism system reduced the free trade and maintain the economy protection in the us capitalist system.

We live in this sigle xxi in an inter-dependent world-that so called globalization.

In competitive today global markets the usa is not alone-so in a mercantil world system, why protection when the free trade bring us the progress. So the us external debt and the export deficit in an economy relation that the government see very good when the economy is selling less and the balance of payment is not equal but in deficit in relation what the government buy and sell that is to say the same in import and export, now in a deficit.

RAFAEL D. MOTA
1-5-16
Brooklyn, new york.

EVALUATION

1.- An monetary spending in import can't be a deficit. but in the buy and loose in relation to the export foreign trade.

2.- proctection economic ideas could be a deficit in import but not in the product sale in the export in the foreing trade.

3.- The balance of payment or the international business balance could do a difference when the country is exporting less in relation to a high import in an economy system.

4.- Industrials needs to export its products, so they need more free trade than protection if are an economic situation that showed that.

5.- Industrials need an economic stimulation in order to improve machinery in an situation of debt an instrumental depreciation, motivated by the benchmark and war.

6.- The us economy is overproducing in a supply economy. If there are an economy speculation in the market and industrials have been goods in the wherehouse, they need the government guarantee to export its products-the DJI shows that the economy is overproducing in the 17.000/000.

7.- The us dollar must continue the FMI rules in order to regulate the new monetary system and the external debt performance (that includes mines in the parity or convertion of the silver and gold-this is very important for the economy health).

8.- With those above follow up end the economic period of 2013-2015-characterized by the US ECONOMIC EXPANSION.

9.- For the period 2016-2017, the US economy enter in the phases cycles. So, we are in recession, the economy is in a GNP economic trend-that means and agree to the phases cycles a next economic step, based in the GNP prosperity, to the another step that must be the recovery and so, so on.

Note: For January 13, 2016. the US economics point out to be in a low GNP trend. Some big companies makes trade this date-so. Seems then the recession start a new stage, with the began of the US economic trend if not recession will continue tending to a financial crash as predicted by some economist.

Rafael d. mota
Brooklyn, n,y,/1/15/16.

GNP ECONOMICS TREND NOTES

In February 19, 2016 the GNP TREND continued with a high interest in the loan by the FEDERAL RESERVE and a Q4 in the monetary policy, the means a reduction in the debts a little be affected the existing inflation. The DJI ALSO CONTINUE IN THE HIGH OF the 16,000 and the technological continue by futhernore in the 4000-so the GNP TREND PROBLEM SEEMS TOBE INTO THE INTERNATIONAL FIELD AND THE s&p index.

In February 8, 2016 Leman and Broders credit bank crisis had been legally resolved. Leman and broders legal credit problemas began in 2007 during the Bush jr. administration.

Also the USA economy was declared in expansion after recession or the called and hoped financial crash the had begin in 2016. So in this year the USA economy will have a new monetary policy about the gold...so the news.

KARL MARX,
ESSENTIAL ECONOMICS
BY RAFAEL D. MOTA

THE CAPITAL II. THE CIRCUIT OF MONEY CAPITAL

CHAPTER I. THE METAMORPHOSIS OF CAPITAL AND CIRCUIT

Marx had three stage of circuit of capital. Those stages are the capital commodity and the labor market. This transform the buy and money in circulation commodities the means money minus capital (M-C) so Marx formula.

The capitalism production and consumption purchase in the function of the capitalist production and commodity are the production capital in the process of the commodity result of the production value of the element of production.

The seller capitalist and commodities are money in circulation that takes way the commodities and money (M-C) so Marx formula.

The circuit of money capital in the Marx formula is like M-C. P. C1-M-4.

The production circuit transform the capital in money and the commodities in production on process of commerce.

This process is interrupted by the capital (C) and money (M) where the capital increase and the money result in surplus value and the means benefits for the capitalist in the form of profits.

THE FIRST STAGE OF THE M-C2

The M-C in the production capital result in money capital in labor production after the labor power, that is shows in the Marx formula of MP. So, the product on sale is the capital money in relation to the production and labor market. The Marx formula for this is M-C=L+MP. It is had a surplus paid by labor in relation to the production organization in the natural value that in the economy is the value of the change of money.

The surplus labor value is paid by the sales wages in the price of products by the hours of selling and buyer. This is circuit of labor hours in price and wages.

The Marx formula for this is: M-C=L+MP. This the Money Value in the Production that is the money production in the labor value (L) or in the production (MP). This is the market supply in the sell and buy value that is the buyer quantity in the money value of the market price.

The much spending in the production and labor mean that that commerce is only necessary in the number of labor. The Marx function of purchase of money capital and payment is the capital circuit in the form of production capital into the production process of the capitalism. The Marx money capital for the circulation of capital is M-C-L. This formula is for the circulation of capital in the purchase of the production of labor and prices. This is the sale of the labor power in the purchase of every sale in the first stage of circulation of the commodity metamorphosis of the transformation of the money form. The spend of money in the consumption is the overall commodity in the circulation of money. The Marx formula for this is C-M-C; L-M(C-M) and M-C and all this in the general form is C-M-C.

The transformation of money capital into production capital is the value of money into the capital value of the production value. This is the transformation for the money into capital, the capitalist production of the labor prices that is the quantity of labor. The price of the labor power or wage in the value of the capitalization Is the surplus value in the form of wages in the labor money production.

The money relation for the purchase appears with the buyer and services that is the revolution of the money capital. The capitalist money of the commodities power is the money sum of the relation of the buyer and seller in the production Of the worker in the labor power.

The capital or the money capital is the commodity in circulation of the purchase and sale of an slavery spending of money. The distribution means consumption in the production of the capitalism surplus value in the circuit of the production capital.

2.-SECOND STAGE. THE FUNCTION OF PRODUCTION CAPITAL

The consolidation of money for the sale effort and commodities is the money transformation In money, production of capital and capital value.

The consume are commodities in the labor power in an economic process of equilibrium in an first stage of the capitalism for an second stage of production.

The labor wage is in relation with the market sale the require of an daily transformation in an firm of labor power for the purchase payment in the labor production.

The capitalist money is used in a thirst production. The wage and labor means a substitution of the purchase,

The commodities of buy and sale is knows as the circulation of products.

The labor power explotation of the economic structure of an capitalism system of an big extension of the technique of production in the extension of value.

THE THIRD SATAGE C1-M2

The production of the money production is the sum of money in gold that is the form of money.

THE FOUR STAGE. THE LABOR AS A WHOLE

When the commodities is bouth in the market and are consume as material and value in the production and capital is the material value in the circulation form. M-V are the supplement C-M in the second stage that in an circulation phase of commodity and value, the value appears transformin a total process in the production circuit.

The industry branch is part of the industrial capital, that basis of the industrial capital. The circuit capital vary the production phase. The cease the stock of the commodities that abstract the flow of circulation.

The value become the production capital of the factories building, machinery among others. The manufacture produce the production its circulation, also the service and the consumption.

The transplant of the industry does not creates new products and the service does not change of place.

THE CIRCUIT OF PRODUCTION CAPITAL

The general productive capital is the reproduction that so Marx formula is: p-c1-m1-c1-c-p. That means a reproduction of the production process and value. This is the function of the capital that is the reproduction of the surplus value. The investment of an industry branch is the labor transformed in value and money, so the capital.

Marx said the "circulation proper appears only as the...reproduction... repeated and made..thought repetition".

The circuit money capital=m-c-m(m-l-l-m)

The value determination=c-m-l(c-m-m-l)

In the form of commodity circulation.

THE SIMPLE REPRODUCTION

C1-M-C is all process of production in the commodity capital that is the formula function of cl-m in the term of the capital value P the exist in the commodity in a second process of a circuit money capital of reproduction. The productive capital of the industry capital is the second value that turn in gold in the general circulation of commodity that is the individual capital that is the capitalist.

The circuit of value in a normal production must be sold in the market the value cl. But the formula c-m-1 represent a change of value in the production relations-a production labor in a capitalist marker system. Marx said "the change of value in a later production factors change it. The reproduction metamorphosis of the commodities process the production as a whole that includes the circulation capital in a specific interchange of material." This change is represented by the Marx formula c-m-c, this also includes the c for the production commodities. The balance of payment is about the seller capitalist in circuit of money that is the capital circulation.

The transformation of the money capital in a commodity purchase in a productive consumption that falls in the circuit capital when it is the surplus value in consume. The exchange of products is in money. For the economist it is not a "possible" overproduction.

The whole circuit production process in an individual capitalist consumption- the worker is conditional from a view considered in crisis. The capitalist production in a scale production needs an expansion that satisfied the supply and demand. The industrial production in a mass or wholsale production, the merchant can get the purchase-so the expansion in a scale production consumption.

THE SECOND STAGE ABOUT ACCUMULATION, REPRODUCTION AND EXPANDED SCALE

The reproduction process can be expanded by the "technical factors". The realization of the capitalism is by the surplus value; the add capital in the circuit of the capital value process. The capital is the number of cuircuits of the money capital. The money capital can't be expanded in the production itself. This needs the sell in gold and silver; the production to the merchant for a national product. This means circulation in the purchase for a hoard distribution. The money sell the capital during the trasactions and this is the circuits of the individual industrial capital.

THE END

NOTE;

In the Capital III, the Capitalist Society as a Whole, Marx try the labor capital and the dependence of the worker of the capital. Also try, the business capital and production in a capitalist society, where from his point of view, the worker is exposed to the capital explotation. So, the worker wages does go out of the capital but the worker produce his own salary. Also, Marx try the capital profit and worker, the creates its own production.

With this note we finished this book called "Karl Marx, Essential Economics" based on the Capital I-II, where the production and the circuit capital is tried-or the is the same "the study of the production and also the study of the commerce" in the capitalist society at that different of the capital III that study, the capitalist society as a whole which mean a study of the wages that become from the production as well as become the profit from the capital created by the worker from production.

APPENDIX

THE SUPPLY ECONOMICS AND A DUMPING POLITICS,

BY: RAFAEL D. MOTA

So, the cnn news on May 13, 2016 in the US NATION is developing an dumping situation, characterized by an external commerce with the emergencies economics.

The following day (during the morning) the news report a drop in the wall street among the DJI, the had a down of little more of 119.00 point, also in the technological markert but most important in the S&P poor the had a down point a little over of 19.00. Seems to me the US nation is faced an international situation created by the monopoly that in the past established an supplied economics in order to makes control of the other market like the ratails store. Today the Nation is facing this international situation after the past economy expansion that was following up of a trade economics were the problem is consisted now on a dumping economies were the monopolies tried by a little time to makes a total control of the markets eliminating the competency of the little businesses-we must remember that the US market was composed by 80% of monopolies and a 20% of ratails or small businesses.

The is bringing consecuencies in the US ECONOMY reflected on the date trade with the down of the wall street, specially in the s&p were the international markets are located.

Now, is the situation that is facing the nation with an international problems that is also affecting the marker prices (now for example Uk is facing a similar situation and also decided to get out of the Union Europe, in the emergencies markets is the case of Brasil were had been a bankbrusep the conclused with desposition of the president lula and russeef and Argentina similar with a corralito situation. In the devepment of Europe Greece is also facing economics problem on the date).

The dumping is an economy law like recessions, depressions, inflation etc. that consist in the competency of the monopolies with the ratails or small markets that affects the prices. And on the date it is the dumping politics the is facing the nation in the trade economics, now in the s&p poor index.

THE US NEW MONETARY SYSTEM

The FMI intervined the US monetary system and put to function a new money different to the all kowns as the US dollar.

By December 7, 2014; 190 countries were in international debt. The US debt was before it with their citizens. But the during the Barack Obama government, the US incurred in an international debt by the date above of 17,997,881,181,468.20.

Four our days the US external debt has increased.

ANNEX

The Monopoly

The United States Corporate profit for the end of the 2009 year in current production with the inventory valuation of capital competition and adjustments, increases $130.00 billion in the third quarter of 2009 year. It is composed for an increase of $43.00 billion in second quarter. The current production in the cash flow; it means the that cash flow increase in inventory valuation adjustments. The cash fund available in corporation for investment increase in $40 billion in the third quarter in contrast to an decrease of $305 billion in the second quarter of 2009.

The tax corporate income increase in $6.7 billion in the third quarter, composed with a income of $35.6 billion for the second quarter of the 2009. Profits after adjustments increases of $123.3 billion for the third quarter of the 2009; composed with an increase of $8.2 billion for the second quarter of the 2009 year.

Comerstar presents for the financial composition increase $97.0 billion in the third quarter with an increase of $28.5 billion in the same quarter. Non functional corporates increased $12.5 billion in the third quarter with an increase of $29.8 billion in the second quarter of the 2009.

For the rest of the world it is composed with an increase of $20.1 billion in the third quarter and an increase of 14.0 billion in the second quarter of the 2009 year. The profits before tax increase in $156.2 billion in the third quarter.

The profits before tax increase in 15.2 billion in the third quarter.

The coporate composition adjustment inconme $9.2 billion in the third quarter. The inventory valuation adjustment decrease $35.5 billion composed with an decrease $35.5 billion; composed also with a decrease of $63.0 billion for the 2009.

For the 2007 the GNP was 706.500. The net domestic product for the 2008 was 102.875 and for the 2009 was $101.400.

The gross domestic product in the same year up was $105.957 in the total.

It was equal to the net nationalproduct of $106.118 in the total for the 2007. Adding for the same year in net domestic product $105.487. In the international arena there are a depending of th fuel imports third brand monopoly regarding Honduras where the coup e'etat Manuel Zelaya is president.

US make coporate enterprises in Central America, Mexico and the Caribbean Where monopoly the banana in Honduras and Central America.

In the same way there is a dependency of 2 trillion barrel of oil from Singapore. The Devon Economy Corporation had agreement with the shell in order to develope a proyet in deep water in the gulf of Mexico to Dinamarca. Based maenst oil for 1.3 billion in Oklahoma company. Tustle composed the dividend counts 50% working in intent with cascade with a 25% for the proyet. That means for them 1.1 billion after take way the taxes. It will be effeive for January 1, and expected for Feb.1 of the 2010. It will be gain yearly 4.5 billion to 7.5 billion.

The corporation are not helping the government in order stimulate the economy crisis but in investment.